First Aid for You

by Rebecca Weber

Content Adviser: September Kirby, CNS, MS, RN,
Instructor, Health Promotion and Wellness,
South Dakota State University

Reading Adviser: Rosemary G. Palmer, Ph.D.,
Department of Literacy, College of Education,
Boise State University

Spyglass BOOKS

COMPASS POINT BOOKS

Minneapolis, Minnesota

Compass Point Books
3109 West 50th Street, #115
Minneapolis, MN 55410

Visit Compass Point Books on the Internet at *www.compasspointbooks.com*
or e-mail your request to *custserv@compasspointbooks.com*

Photographs ©: Digital Vision, cover, 16; Image Ideas, 4, 14; David Falconer, 5 (left); Phil
Bulgach, 5 (right); Bruce Coleman, Inc./Keith Gunnar, 6; Bruce Coleman, Inc./Ken Lax, 7;
DAVID R. FRAZIER Photolibrary, 8, 18; Chuck Savage/Corbis, 9; Comstock, 10, 21
(middle and bottom); John Easley/Deep Sea Images, 11, 12; Paul Osmond/Deep Sea Images, 13;
Bruce Coleman, Inc./L. West, 15; PhotoDisc, 17; Rob Lewine/Corbis, 19; EyeWire, 20, 21 (top).

Editor: Patricia Stockland
Photo Researcher: Marcie C. Spence
Designer: Jaime Martens

Library of Congress has cataloged the hardcover edition as follows:
Weber, Rebecca.
  First aid for you / by Rebecca Weber.
      p. cm. — (Spyglass books)
  Includes bibliographical references and index.
  Contents: You can help—Cuts and scrapes—Choking—Bites and stings—Broken bones.
  ISBN 0-7565-0623-9 (hardcover)
  1. First aid in illness and injury—Juvenile literature. 2. Medical emergencies—Juvenile literature.
  [1. First aid.] I. Title. II. Series.
  RC86.5.W42 2004
  616.02'52—dc22   2003014478

  ISBN 0-7565-0926-2 First printing in paperback, 2005

Contents

NOTE: Glossary words are in *bold* the first time they appear.

You Can Help

Each day, people do many things. Sometimes *accidents* happen. People may get hurt. People may get sick. You may be able to help.

The Number to Call

If someone is badly hurt or in danger, dial 911. Tell them the problem. Firefighters and police officers will be there in minutes.

5

Cuts and Scrapes

If someone is cut or
scraped, you can help.
First, look to see how
badly the person is hurt.
If a cut is bleeding,
call an adult for help.

Then, hold a clean cloth over the cut. Keep holding the cloth until the bleeding stops.

Leave the cloth in one place. If you move it, the bleeding could start again.

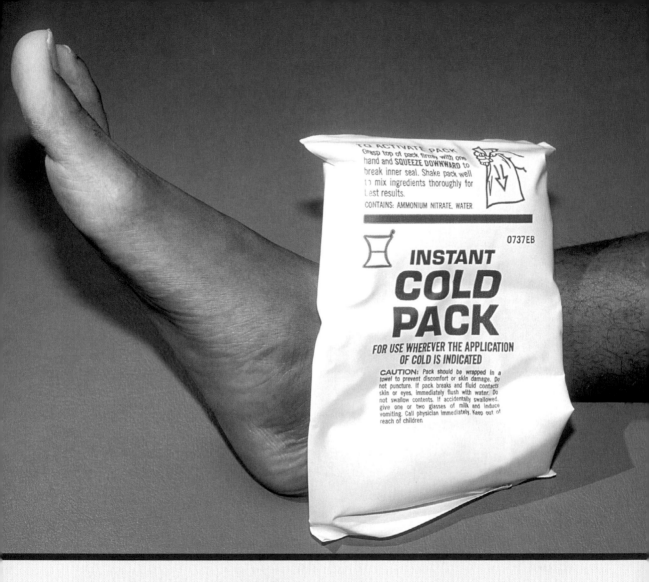

A Cool Idea

Put an *ice pack* over a bandage.
It can slow down or stop bleeding.
A bag of frozen vegetables makes
a great ice pack!

Nosebleeds

A person might get a nosebleed. Have the person lean forward. Pinch the soft part of the nose for 10 full minutes. Do not let go until the bleeding stops.

9

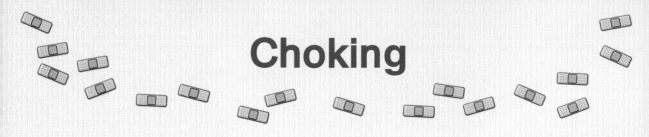

Choking

If someone is choking, you can help.

First, find out if the person can make any mouth sounds. If not, call 911.

An adult may do the Heimlich maneuver. She wraps her arms around the person's middle. Then she quickly pulls her hands back and up. This makes the object come out.

Sounds Are Good News

If a person who is choking can talk or cough, she doesn't need help. A person who can't make sounds can't breathe. This person needs help fast.

12

Hit the Spot

Sometimes the food can be knocked loose. Just have an adult hit the middle of the person's back.

13

Bites and Stings

If someone has been
bitten, you can help.

First, make sure there is
no danger. Call 911 if you
can't get close enough
to help.

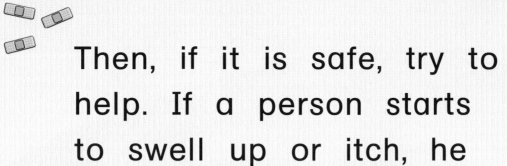

Then, if it is safe, try to help. If a person starts to swell up or itch, he may have an *allergy.* Call for help.

Some bites and stings are just painful. Leave them alone. Press a clean cloth to wounds that are bleeding.

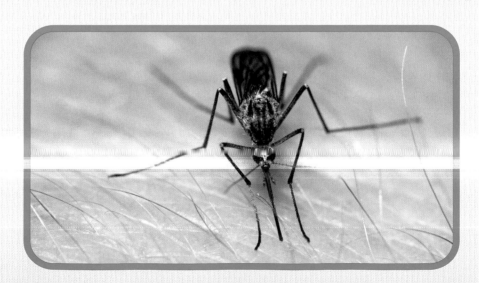

Bad Bites

A bite from a person can be **dangerous**, too! People's mouths have many *germs.* Someone who is bitten by another person should see a doctor.

Animal Actions

Even friendly animals may bite.
Leave animals alone when they are
eating or sleeping. Also, never go
near animals you don't know.

Broken Bones

If you think someone has a broken bone, call 911 for help.

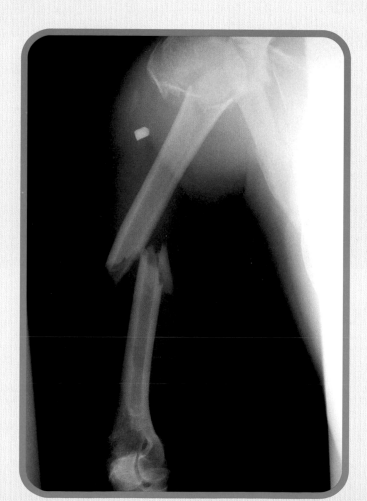

Stay Still

Do not move the person unless he is in danger. Moving could make the broken bone worse. Keep him quiet and still until help arrives. You have helped!

19

Make a First Aid Kit

It is always a good idea to have a first aid kit. Have an adult help you put one together. Every kit should have:

- ✔ bandages of different sizes
- ✔ *gauze* pads and rolls of gauze
- ✔ bandage tape
- ✔ elastic bandages
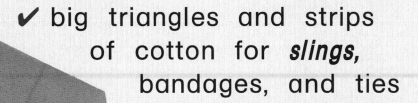
- ✔ big triangles and strips of cotton for *slings,* bandages, and ties
- ✔ cotton balls
- ✔ tissues or a roll of toilet paper
- ✔ safety pins, scissors, and tweezers
- ✔ thermometer
- ✔ antibiotic cream and hydrogen peroxide

98.6

Glossary

accident–something that was not
　　supposed to happen

allergy–a body's sensitivity to things
　　like stings or food that causes
　　sneezing, swelling, coughing,
　　or sickness

dangerous–something that may cause
　　hurt or harm

gauze–light and loosely woven cloth

germs–tiny organisms that make you sick

ice pack–a bag that is filled with ice

sling–a strip of cloth that holds an
　　injured arm in one place

Learn More

Books

Gale, Karen Buhler. Illustrated by Michael Kline. *The Kids' Guide to First Aid: All About Bruises, Burns, Stings, Sprains & Other Ouches.* Charlotte, VT: Williamson Pub., 2002.

On the Web

For more information on First Aid for You, use FactHound to track down Web sites related to this book.

1. Go to *www.compasspointbooks.com/ facthound*
2. Type in this book ID: 0756506239
3. Click on the *Fetch It* button. Your trusty FactHound will fetch the best Web sites for you!

Index

GR: H
Word Count: 216

From Rebecca Weber

The world is such a great place! I love teaching kids how to take care of themselves and take care of nature.